American Art Association

High-class paintings

many of which are by the great modern masters

American Art Association

High-class paintings
many of which are by the great modern masters

ISBN/EAN: 9783744650502

Printed in Europe, USA, Canada, Australia, Japan

Cover: Foto ©Thomas Meinert / pixelio.de

More available books at **www.hansebooks.com**

CATALOGUE

OF

HIGH-CLASS PAINTINGS

MANY OF WHICH ARE BY THE

Great Modern Masters

Private Collection of

MR. HENRY PROBASCO

Cincinnati, Ohio

TO BE SOLD BY AUCTION, WITHOUT RESERVE

On Monday Evening, April Eighteenth,

Beginning at 7.30 o'clock prompt

At Chickering Hall

Fifth Avenue and Eighteenth Street

THE COLLECTION WILL BE ON EXHIBITION

Day and Evening

At the American Art Galleries

From Saturday, April Ninth, until date of sale inclusive

(Sundays excepted)

AMERICAN ART ASSOCIATION, Managers

THOMAS E. KIRBY, Auctioneer

1887

CONDITIONS OF SALE

1. The highest Bidder to be the Buyer, and if any dispute arise between two or more Bidders, the Lot so in dispute shall be immediately put up again and re-sold.

2. The Purchasers to give their names and addresses, and to pay down a cash deposit, or the whole of the Purchase-money, if required ; in default of which, the Lot or Lots so purchased to be immediately put up again and re-sold.

3. The Lots to be taken away at the Buyer's Expense and Risk on the morning following each session of the Sale, between 9 and 12 o'clock, and the remainder of the Purchase-money to be absolutely paid, or otherwise settled for to the satisfaction of the Auctioneer, on or before delivery ; in default of which, the undersigned will not hold himself responsible if the Lots be lost, stolen, damaged, or destroyed, but they will be left at the sole risk of the Purchaser.

4. The sale of any Painting or other object is not to be set aside on account of any error in the description or defect. All are exposed for Public Exhibition one or more days, and are sold just as they are, without recourse.

5. To prevent inaccuracy in delivery and inconvenience in the settlement of the Purchases, no Lot can, on any account, be removed during the Sale.

6. Upon failure to comply with the above conditions, the money deposited in part payment shall be forfeited ; all Lots uncleared within the time aforesaid shall be re-sold by public or private Sale, without further notice, and the deficiency (if any) attending such re-sale shall be made good by the defaulter at this Sale, together with all charges attending the same. This condition is without prejudice to the right of the Auctioneer to enforce the contract made at this Sale, without such re-sale, if he thinks fit.

THOMAS E. KIRBY, Auctioneer

SPECIAL NOTICE

ORDERS TO PURCHASE

The undersigned will receive and attend to orders to purchase at this sale :

Messrs. M. KNOEDLER & CO., *Fifth Avenue and 22d Street.*

Mr. L. CRIST DELMONICO (*Kohn's Art Rooms*), *No. 166 Fifth Avenue.*

Messrs. BLAKESLEE & CO., *cor. Fifth Avenue and 26th Street.*

Mr. WILLIAM SCHAUS, *No. 204 Fifth Avenue.*

Messrs. REICHARD & CO., *No. 226 Fifth Avenue.*

Messrs. EDGAR S. ALLIEN & CO., *No. 174 Fifth Avenue.*

Mr. L. A. LANTHIER, *No. 22 East 16th Street.*

Mr. PETER BRETT, *Room 449, Produce Exchange.*

Messrs. ORTGIES & CO., *Nos. 845 and 847 Broadway.*

AMERICAN ART ASSOCIATION, *No. 6 East 23d Street.*

No. 27. Norwegian Landscape.
Baron F. J. Hendriks.

CATALOGUE

** Measurements given are in inches, the first figures indicating the width of Canvas or Panel

No. 1

Confidence

13 x 16.   Dated 1856

FLORENT WILLEMS,   .   Paris

Born at Luttich, January 8, 1823.   Medals, at Paris, 1844. 1846, 1855; at Brussels, 1843.   Chevalier and Officer of the Order of Leopold and Legion of Honor.   Medal (Exposition Universelle), 1867.   First class Medal (Exposition Universelle), 1878.

No. 2   .

The Young Mother

11 x 14

J. B. J. TRAYER,   Paris

Born in 1824 at Paris.   Studied with his father and with Lequieus. Medals, Paris, 1853 and 1855.

No. 3

The Consultation

17 x 13. Dated 1866

WILHELM SOHN,   *Düsseldorf*

*Born in 1830 at Berlin. Came in 1847 to Düsseldorf, where he studied
with his uncle, Karl Sohn, whose daughter he afterward married.
In 1874 he accepted the position of Professor at the Academy in
Düsseldorf. Medal, 1867.*

No. 4

Bull, Sheep and Goats

64 x 43

LOUIS ROBBE, ... *Brussels*

*Born November 17, 1806, at Courtray, Belgium. Was at first a lawyer
(1830) in Ghent, and in 1840 one of the syndics of Brussels. He
entered the academy of his native town, and in a few years had
earned many medals and other honors. In 1844 he was made a
Knight of the Spanish Order of Charles III.; in 1845 a Knight of
the Legion of Honor, and in 1863 an officer of the Belgian Order of
Leopold.*

No. 5

Grandfather's Birthday

34 x 26. Dated 1854

J. P. HASENCLEVER, . . *Düsseldorf*

*Born at Remscheid, near Solingen, May 18, 1810. Pupil of Schadow.
Member of Berlin, Düsseldorf, and Amsterdam Academies. Gold
medal at Brussels. Died at Düsseldorf, December 16, 1863.*

No. 19 Landscape.—Cattle and Dog.

MR. Marie Rosa Bonheur.

No. 4.   Bull, Sheep, and Goats.
Louis Robbe.

No. 50.   The New Robe.
Alfred Stevens.

No. 6

Norwegian Landscape

42 x 33. Dated 1856

HANS FREDERICK GUDE, Düsseldorf

*Born in Christiania, 1825. Pupil of Andreas Achenbach and of Düssel-
dorf Academy, under Schirmer. Professor of same institution in
1854, of Art School at Carlsruhe in 1864, and of Berlin Academy in
1880. Member of Amsterdam, Rotterdam, Stockholm, Berlin, and
Vienna Academies. Great Gold Medal in Berlin, 1852 and 1860,
and Weimar, 1861. Medals, Paris, 1855, 1861, 1867.*

No. 7

Reverie

13 x 19

JEAN ERNEST AUBERT, . Paris

*Born at Paris, 1824. Pupil of Paul Delaroche, and in engraving of
Martinet; won the prix de Rome for engraving in 1844. Medals
for painting, Paris, 1861, 1878.*

No. 8

The Convalescent

(Sairey Gamp and Betsy Prig)

11 x 9. Dated 1865

A. H. BAKKER-KORFF, The Hague

*Born at The Hague, August 31, 1824. Pupil of The Hague Academy, of
Kruseman, and J. E. J. van den Berg. Died in Leyden, 1882.*

No. 9

Summer Landscape

J. T 21

THÉODORE ROUSSEAU,   *Paris*

*Born in Paris, 1812. Pupil of Guillon-Lethiere. First exhibited,
Salon, 1834. Medals, 1834, 1840, 1855. Legion of Honor, 1852.
One of the eight Grand Medals of Honor (Exposition Universelle),
Paris, 1867. Died, 1867. Diploma to the Memory of Deceased
Artists, 1868.*

Extracts from Notes Sur les Cent Chefs-d'Œuvres, by M. Albert Wolff.

*In that group of landscape painters of foremost rank whose destiny
was to restore modern art in France to the magnificent position of
RUYSDAËL and HOBBEMA, THÉODORE ROUSSEAU is unquestionably
the one who has gone farthest into the secret of nature. To be just,
JULES DUPRÉ had pointed him the way; but, when once launched,
ROUSSEAU had separated from his comrade to pursue his own des-
tinies. A love for nature had been formed in this tailor's son in
the humble position which he occupied with one of his relations who
had a saw factory in Franche-Comté. While accompanying his
employer in his professional tours in search of growing timber, this
youth, among the trees, came to catch the scent of the grand principles of art, of that theory on which was to rise, later, the mighty
scaffold of his renown. When he got leave to follow his bent, at
the age of fifteen years, THÉODORE ROUSSEAU was confided to an
indifferent artist named RÉMOND, who passed for the foremost landscape painter of the time. He was taught what was then called
grand art, the kind of "historical" landscape where figures of the
Bible or of ancient history strayed through conventional scenery.
Those proud ones of 1820, those forgotten ones to-day, took no
notice of the vegetation which surrounded them or of the contemporary figures circulating through it. There would not be kept a single
memory of those painters now were it not for a ROUSSEAU, a DU-
PRÉ, a COROT, a DELACROIX, a MILLET, who suffered by them, and
whose hapless story cannot be related without at least citing the
names of the professional ancestors who preceded our group of*

No. 20. Landscape and Cattle, Early Morning.
F. A. Bonheur.

No. 14. The Musicians.
H. C. A. Baron.

No. 13. Stable Interior.
Franz Adam

giants. In his hours of freedom, the young THÉODORE ROUSSEAU
would forget the ill teaching of his master before the instruction
derived from the external creation. It may be claimed for him that
he was the pet pupil of nature, and a grateful and sensitive pupil,
who began to consecrate a lifetime thenceforth to glorifying his
benefactress. It was in the environs of Paris that young ROUS-
SEAU would temper his soul after the deleterious lessons that were
sought to be forced on him. The illustrious RÉMOND lost his time
when he endeavored to convince this particular scholar that it was
necessary to pass by, with calm and haughty indifference, before the
splendors of creation and contrive an art out of counterfeit.

For THÉODORE ROUSSEAU the feeling for veritable art was accompanied by a profound love of his native soil. It seemed to him that
France was sufficiently rich in picturesque sites to inspire a painter.
Did not RUYSDAEL derive a part of his quality from the very fact
that it is the aspect of his own country which his art celebrates?
Was not HOBBEMA an immortal landscape painter especially because he had developed his genius by the tender study of the land
where he was born? Was it not mere foolhardiness to try to con-
struct by theory a world more fine than the actual world, to disdain
the glories of our forests, the beauties of our plains, to go astray in
the vagaries of rearrangements of foliage such as was never seen
but in the pictures of our forefathers? It was an inexplicable
thing to the young ROUSSEAU that these blind eyes could see nothing
of the splendors which surrounded them. What, did their hearts
never beat, did they not feel the intoxication of nature which stirred
the blood of this stripling? Their artificial painting was without
soul, without emotion; the grandeurs of their native soil escaped
them; the poesy of our forests remained for them a sealed book;
these men had never thrilled to the scenery of home. And they
called themselves artists!

At the period of the French Restoration, the painters of England were
the first to rise in revolt against the successful routine of historical
landscape. But their works were unknown in France; it cannot,
then, be said that they showed the road to the great French landscape artists; they arose but a short time before our own; they
emerged, as ours did, from the protest of all honest hearts against
the artificial. The instinct of truth and the need to strike deep into
nature are innate in humanity. Separated by the ocean and knowing
nothing of each other, the English and the French marched by two
different paths toward the same end. In this awakening of a sin-

cere art in either country, France was destined to place herself at last in the first rank, and leave far behind her the English school. Among the great French landscape painters who have not only guided the national art back again to nature, but whose influence was to be so important over the foreign schools, THÉODORE ROUS-SEAU occupies the highest place, because he is the most perfect master. The grand aspects of landscape and its tenderness are equally familiar to him. He renders with the same mastery the smile of creation and its terrors, the broad, open plain and the mysterious forest, the limpid, sunbright sky or the heaping of the clouds put to flight by storms, the terrible aspects of landscape or those replete with grace. He has understood all, rendered all with equal genius. The great contemporary painters have each a particular stamp, COROT painting the grace, MILLET the hidden voice, JULES DUPRÉ the majestic strength, THÉODORE ROUSSEAU has been by turns as much a poet as COROT, as melancholy as MILLET, as awful as DUPRÉ; he is the most complete, for he embraces landscape art absolutely.

No. 10

The Musical Schoolmaster

36 x 28.   Dated 1855

F. DE BRAEKELEER, .   . Antwerp

Born in Antwerp, February 19, 1792.   Pupil of Antwerp Academy and of M. I. Van Brée.   Obtained the great prize in 1819, and studied three years in Rome.   Member of the Order of Leopold, and director of Antwerp Museum   Died 1883.

No. 11

Confidence

11 x 14

CHARLES F. PÉCRUS, .   . Paris

No. 23. Landscape.
Jules Dupré.

No. 5. Landscape, Cattle and Figures.
E. J. Verboeckhoven and J. A. Achard.

No. 12. Landscape.
B. C. Koek-Koek.

No. 12

Landscape

17 x 13

B. C. KOEK-KOEK, . . . *Amsterdam*

Born at Middelburg, Zealand, October 11, 1803, died at Cleves, April 5, 1862. Son and pupil of Johannes Hermanus Koek-Koek, marine painter, and student of the Amsterdam Academy under Schelfhout and Van Os, founder of the Academy of Design at Cleves, member of Rotterdam and St. Petersburg Academies, member of the Orders of the Lion and of Leopold. Legion of Honor, 1840. Gold medals, at Amsterdam, 1840, Paris, 1840 and 1843.

No. 13

Stable Interior

46 x 56

FRANZ ADAM, *Munich*

Born at Milan, May 4, 1815. Pupil of Albrecht, member of Munich and Vienna Academies; Order of St. Michael. Great Gold Medal at Berlin, 1875.

No. 14

The Musicians

18 x 24

HENRI C. A. BARON, . *Paris*

Born at Besançon, June, 1816. Pupil of Gignoux, made his début in the Salon in 1840, then visited Italy. Medals, 1847, 1848, 1865, 1867. Member of the Legion of Honor, 1859.

No. 15

Return from the Alps

29 x 20. Dated 1837

HEINRICH BÜRKEL, . . . Munich

Born at Pirmasenz, Rhenish Palatinate, May 29, 1802, died in Munich, June 10, 1869. Pupil of Munich Academy, but mostly formed himself, studying and copying the Dutch masters in the Munich and Schleissheim Galleries. Was honorary member of the Munich, Dresden, and Vienna Academies.

No. 16

The Happy Mother

13 x 17

E. F. DE BLOCK, . Antwerp

Born at Grammont, East Flanders, May 14, 1812. Pupil, at Ghent, of Van Huffel, and in Antwerp, of Braekeleer. Medal, Paris, 1842. Legion of Honor, 1846.

No. 17

Roman Peasant Girl Asleep

17 x 13. Dated 1856

LÉON J. F. BONNAT, . Paris

Born at Bayonne in 1833. Pupil, in Madrid, of F. de Madrazo, in Paris, of Léon Cogniet; also studied four years in Italy, where he painted many small pictures of Italian life. Has painted several religious pictures for the Government. Second grand prix, 1858; medals, 1861, 1863, and 1869. Member of the Legion of Honor, 1867, officer of the same, 1874, commander, 1882. Member of the Institute of France.

No. 14. Landscape—Harvest Time.

J. Linnell, Sr.

No. 24.   A Mother's Pride.
Auguste Delacroix.

No. 43.   The Golden Wedding.
F. De Braekeleer.

No. 18

In the Dog Kennel—Early Morning

18 x 21. Dated 1867

JEAN MAXIME CLAUDE, . Paris

Born in Paris, June 24, 1824. Pupil of Galland. Medals, 1866, 1869, and 1872.

No. 19

Landscape, Cattle and Dog

26 x 20. Dated 1867

MLLE. MARIE ROSA BONHEUR,
Paris

Born at Bordeaux, March 22, 1822. Pupil of her father, Raymond B. Bonheur. Began by copying in the Louvre, afterward made studies and sketches near Paris. Her first two pictures, exhibited at Bordeaux, 1841, attracted much attention, and were followed by others which established her world-wide fame. During the Franco-Prussian War, her studio and residence were respected by special order of the Crown Prince of Prussia. Since 1849 she has been director of the Paris Free School of Design for Young Girls, which she founded. Elected member of Antwerp Institute in 1868. Medals, 1845, 1848, 1855, 1867 (Exposition Universelle). Legion of Honor, 1865. Leopold Cross, 1880. Commander's Cross of Royal Order of Isabella the Catholic, 1880.

No. 20

Early Morning—Landscape and Cattle

40 x 25.   Dated 1866

Original study for the " Environs of Fontainbleau," A. T. Stewart Collection.

FRANÇOIS AUGUSTE BONHEUR,
Paris

Born in Bordeaux, November 4, 1824.   Son and pupil of Raymond R.
Bonheur, who died 1853.   Brother of Mlle. Marie Rosa Bonheur.
Medals, Paris, 1852, 1857, 1859, 1861, and 1863.   Member of the
Legion of Honor, 1867.   Died, February, 1884.

No. 21

Swiss Landscape

11 x 9

ALEXANDER CALAME, .   . Paris

Born at Vevay, 1810.   Pupil of Diday.   Medals, Paris, 1839, 1840.
Legion of Honor, 1842.   Member of St. Petersburg and Brussels
Academies.   Died, 1864.

No. 22

Girl and Butterfly

10 x 14

GEORGE BROMLEY, .   London

No. 76. Old Letters.

J. G. Meyer Von Bremen.

No. 65. Our Little Family.
F. E. Meyerheim.

No. 35. Penelope.
C. F. Marchal.

No. 48. Watering the Horses.
W. Verschuur, Sr.

No. 23

Landscape

15 x 10

JULES DUPRÉ, .　　　*Paris*

*Born in Nantes, 1812. As a boy he studied design in the porcelain
manufactory of his father, but soon turned his attention to landscape painting, and made his début in the Salon of 1831. Medals,
Paris, 1833. Legion of Honor, 1849. Medals (Exposition Universelle), 1867. Officer of the Legion of Honor, 1870.*

Extracts from Notes Sur les Cent Chefs-d'Œuvres, by M. Albert Wolff.

*How has this humble porcelain painter arrived at the position of an
important master without having ever been the pupil of any one?
How was the ambition born in that young, infantine brain of twelve
years to bear back landscape art to the magnificence of a* Claude
Lorraine, *of a* Ruysdael, *of a* Hobbema, *before hearing these
names pronounced and without acquaintance with a single one of
their works? It was in the contemplation of nature, in his isola-
tion amidst her influences, that the mind of the lad was open to her
beauty, and that her mystery was sounded by his thought. In his
hours of freedom the boy used to wander over the fields with sketch-
book and pencil. No professor interposed himself between this
talent in its birth and what it portrayed to dictate any narrow
formula. What he was ignorant of he asked but of her; what he
learned was from her teaching. At eighteen, the little china
painter had become a young master. The crayon studies which the
great artist to-day preserves from his early years are so many sur-
prises; for they bear witness to a comprehension of nature unique
for so young a man. In his odd hours, to add to his resources, he
turned out for a friend of the family a series of clock faces, autom-
ata in which, by means of springs connected with the movement,
a sailboat would shoot the arch of a bridge or a hermit ring his
bell from hour to hour. From these low beginnings emerged our
grand artist, solely by the influence of nature.*

*The art of landscape painting was at that time lost in France. It was
despised as a thing of subaltern rank; and this prejudice, notwith-*

*standing the glory which the French school derives from its illustri-
ous landscape painters of the present century, continues still in the
circles of official teaching to such a point that none of the glorious
French landscape artists have been awarded the Salon medal of
honor. True, they have given it themselves with their own hands in
the sight of posterity by their proud, fine, lasting performance. What
added still more to the contempt felt for landscape under the Restoration was, that it had fallen into the hands of the pigmies. When
these subalterns were not occupied in servilely carrying on the style
of POUSSIN, whom they quietly imitated as if that painter had not
himself borne his own style to its conclusion, they pieced out pictures from fragments of their own sketches, as a harlequin costume
is made with rags of every color. In summer they went off for a
booty of sketches, and in winter they stitched these studies together,
and made of them compositions stuffed with broken stumps of trees,
burst arches of bridges, waterfalls and precipices. From top to
bottom the canvas was piled with motivi; it was like a card of pat-
terns of everything that the artist was able to collect on a canvas,
but where there lacked all emotion in the presence of nature—a
matter which some of the painters had never felt, and which the
others spilled on the road in passing from the country whence they
fetched their sketches to the city where they made them into pictures. The young DUPRÉ said to himself, very justly, that since a
painter would be nearer to accuracy in carrying out his work in
the presence of the scene, it would be a good thing to produce pictures entirely copied from nature, in order that they might catch the
stamp of feeling and sincerity. The day when he hit upon this
profession of faith, JULES DUPRÉ indicated for the French school
the road to follow; he was the pathfinder of modern art, as he is
now its illustrious, respected veteran.*

*It was the DUC DE NEMOURS who bought the first picture sent to the
Salon by JULES DUPRÉ. The sale made a great noise; this son of a
king paid twelve hundred francs for the work; for the young
painter it was substantially the assurance of fortune, and at the
same time the official consecration of a career. The revolution of
February sent the duke into exile. The third republic gave him his
country again. Among the first visitors who came to present their
respects to the duke on his return to France was JULES DUPRÉ. The
prince and the painter looked at each other for some moments, to
measure the time passed since their separation by each other's
wrinkled foreheads and whitened hairs.*

No. 41   Landscape, Bull and Dog.

J. K. Heegaard

No. 40. Far from Home.
Ernst Bosch.

No. 30. Quarrelsome Terriers.
F. S. Lachenwitz.

"*Monseigneur,*" *said the artist, with emotion, " I can never forget that my first encouragement came from your royal highness.*"

" *I still keep your picture,*" *answered the prince, " let us come and see it.*"

The canvas was in fact found in the duchess' salon. In this room the duke, taking the artist's arm, said :

"*Your art is happier than either of us, for it has not grown old.*"

The duke had truly spoken. It is the work that leans directly on nature which can outlast the fashions. The revolution of February plunged the artist again into oblivion, just as his future opened smiling before him. JULES DUPRÉ had received two important orders, one from the Government and the other from the DUC D'ORLÉANS, when the revolution broke out. The two pictures, sketched out, remain in the artist's studio. He has frequently of late years been offered enormous sums if he would agree to finish them; but the old master, still independent as in the day of his youth, would be powerless to execute any work to order.

To-day, as forty years ago, he only paints what is in his thoughts. He is always the same proud artist who, having gone to housekeeping with forty thousand francs of debts, rejected the offer of a merchant who engaged in writing to liquidate these old obligations provided the artist would engage to make some concessions to public taste. JULES DUPRÉ remained hesitating an instant; he seemed by a glance to ask the advice of his wife; the latter, worthy of such an artist, understood him and replied :

"*Refuse ! We shall pay our debts slowly, in time.*"

The debts are long since paid. A competence has crowned the faith of the brave household. Children have been reared, and their future is assured. Old age has shown a pleasant face to JULES DUPRÉ, and none more than he has deserved the peace of the latter years.

The amount of his works is great. Sustained compositions, like The Pasture, are numerous; the masterpieces count by dozens. The Luxembourg Gallery owns two admirable canvases by the painter; no collection worthy of the name can be imagined without a picture by JULES DUPRÉ ; the more remarkable have been sold for a bit of bread. The Pasture, representing ten months of toil before nature, was purchased for two thousand francs. Le Vanne, that magnificent canvas owned by M. VAN PRAET, Minister of the Household to the King of the Belgians, brought three thousand. But what was the amount to him ? The money was not an end, but a means to go and work in the presence of nature. He borrowed from the usurers to be able to keep away from the city.

JULES DUPRÉ had hired, at four hundred francs a year, a working-room in the Abbey of Saint-Pierre, in the midst of the forest of Fontainebleau. He came but rarely to Paris, and then on his friends' affairs rather than on his own. It was he who forced ROUSSEAU on the merchants. It was he, too, who peddled the despised works of MILLET among a few collectors of his acquaintance, and who divined TROYON and protected him. He always fled the great city; he regained the solitude of the fields, which had become a necessity. Only the country could restore him the serenity of his thoughts. He returned untiringly to l'Isle-Adam, the region of his early infancy, where he recaptured the enthusiasms of youth. These lovely banks of the Oise have always attracted the painters. THÉODORE ROUSSEAU long lived beside DUPRÉ at l'Isle-Adam. DAUBIGNY was not far away at Auvers. COROT gave his kindly smile and his cheerful song, from time to time, to DUPRÉ, whom he finally termed the BEETHOVEN of landscape. And truly, if the canvases of COROT recalled the adagios of MOZART, the energetic and often terrible subjects of DUPRÉ produced the effect of the symphonies of the immortal BEETHOVEN. Like him, the great landscape painter has invented a new sonorous quality, and has thrown aside the old methods to arrive at the maximum of intensity in his art. The clouds swept by tempests career over the works of DUPRÉ with the vehemence which BEETHOVEN employed when he let loose his orchestra. The landscape artist has constructed on the grand scale, like the musician, in the same rank of ideas, and with the same impetuosity in going to work. The characteristic mark of the productions of DUPRÉ is power arrived at its highest expression. No master has more energetically rendered the rumbling, threatening voices of nature, its overwhelming effects, before which we collect ourselves, humbled and pensive, as we plunge our thoughts in a symphony of BEETHOVEN.

The porcelain painter's apprentice of sixty years ago has likewise managed to perfect his literary education, which was neglected among the necessities of his early years. The works of the great writers are familiar to him, as if he had passed his whole life in examining them. He is fond of quoting in conversation the axioms of one author after another, whence he has derived the principles of his own peculiar art. To a purchaser who was teasing him to finish a picture in a few hours, with the aid of that sureness of hand and eye which he has acquired, JULES DUPRÉ replied in my presence:

No. 44. Autumn's Golden Crown.
Vicat Cole.

No. 58. Flowers.
George Harrison.

No. 57. Winter Sport.
Carl Hilvers.

"You think, then, that I know my profession? Why, my poor fellow, if I had nothing more to find out and to learn, I could not paint any longer."

In these words is his whole life of search and study. Truly, the day when self-doubt should vanish from an artist's mind, the day when he should not feel before his canvas the trouble which throws the brain into fever, on that day he would be no better than a workman taking up in the morning the task of the evening before, ploddingly and without hesitation, but also without mobility. The day when JULES DUPRÉ should open his studio without a thrill and leave it without discouragement, he would consider that he had arrived at the end of what he could do—and he would be right.

No. 24

A Mother's Pride

22 x 27

AUGUSTE DELACROIX, . Paris

Born at Boulogne-sur-Mer, January 27, 1809, died there November, 1868. Paralyzed during several years before his death, he painted his last works with his left hand. Medals, 1839, 1841, 1846.

No. 25

The Christmas Fair

14 x 18.   Dated 1856

EDUARD GESELSCHAP, . Düsseldorf

Born in Amsterdam, March 22, 1814, died in Düsseldorf, January 5, 1878. Pupil in Wesel of Welsch, then in 1834-41 of Düsseldorf Academy under Schadow; member of the Amsterdam Academy.

No. 26

Memnon at Thebes

40 x 30.   Dated 1845

(Painted for Professor Lepsius in Egypt)

JOHANNES FREY,   Basle

Born at Basle in 1813, died at Frascati, near Rome, in 1865.   Studied principally in Italy; in 1842 he accompanied Professor Lepsius to Egypt, whence, on his return in 1843, he brought many excellent sketches.

No. 27

Norwegian Landscape

50 x 34

BARON F. HENDRIK,   .   Arnheim

Born at Arnheim, 1868.

No. 28

Sunset off the Isle of Jersey

46 x 32

EDUARD HILDEBRANDT,   Berlin

Born in Dantzic, September 9, 1817, died in Berlin, October 25, 1868. Pupil in Berlin of Krause, and in 1841–43 in Paris of Isabey. Went around the world in 1862–64, and brought home 300 water-colors, which, when exhibited in London in 1866, attracted much attention.   In 1853, was made Professor of Berlin Academy.

No. 46. Russian Landscape—Horses and Figures

Adolphe Schreyer.

No. 79. Florentine Flower Girl.
M. Gordigiani.

No. 71. The Disputed Bonnet.
Chas. Verlat.

No. 29

Landscape—Harvest Time

40 x 28. Dated 1863

JOHN LINNELL, SR., London

Born in London, June 16, 1792, died at Redhill, near London, January 20, 1882. Pupil of Benjamin West, John Varley, and of the Royal Academy.

No. 30

Quarrelsome Terriers

28 x 22

SIGMUND LACHENWITZ, Düsseldorf

Born at Neuss in 1820, died in Düsseldorf, June 25, 1868. Pupil of Düsseldorf Academy.

No. 31

A Savoyard

15 x 21. Dated 1866

A. A. E. HÉBERT, Paris

Born at Grenoble, November 3, 1817. Pupil of David d'Angers and Paul Delaroche. Abandoned the law for painting on account of the success of a picture sent to the Salon, which was bought by the Government. Won the grand prix de Rome in 1839; made repeated visits to Italy; medals, 1851, 1855, 1867. Member of the Legion of Honor, 1853; officer of the same, 1867; commander, 1874. Member of the Institute of France, director of the French School of Art in Rome from 1866 to 1873, and again in 1885.

No. 32

Landscape

25 x 20

ADOLPHE WEBER,   . Düsseldorf

Born at Frankfort, 1817, died 1873. Pupil of Rosenkranz and Schilbach.

No. 33

Landscape, Cattle and Figures

40 x 28. Dated 1865

E. J. VERBOECKHOVEN,   . Brussels
JEAN ALEXIS ACHARD,   Paris

Verboeckhoven was born at Warneton (West Flanders), July 8, 1799. Medals at Paris, 1824, 1841, 1855. Legion of Honor, 1845. Chevalier of the Orders of Leopold, St. Michael of Bavaria, and Christ of Portugal. Decoration of the Iron Cross. Member of the Royal Academies of Belgium, Antwerp, and St. Petersburg. Died, 1881. Achard was born at Voreppe, Isère, France, June 8, 1807, died in Grenoble, October, 1884. Landscape painter, self-taught; went to Paris in 1835. Medals, 1844, 1845, 1848, 1855.

No. 34

The Card Houses

34 x 26. Dated 1859

AUGUSTE TOULMOUCHE,   Paris

Born at Nantes in 1829. Pupil of Gleyre. Medals, Paris, 1852, 1859, 1861, 1878. Legion of Honor, 1870.

No. 52. Vision of St. Hubertus.
Theodore Budde.

No. 82. Avenue of Beeches—Winter, The Hague.
De Meyer.

No. 35

Penelope

20 x 40. Dated 1868

CHARLES F. MARCHAL,   Paris

Born in Paris, 1825, died there March 31, 1877. Pupil of Drölling and Dubois. Improved and prospered until 1876, when he lost his eyesight, and in despair committed suicide. Medals, 1864, 1866, and 1873.

No. 36

Old Letters

15 x 20. Dated 1867

J. G. MEYER, VON BREMEN, Berlin

Called, from his birthplace, Meyer von Bremen. Born October 28, 1813. Pupil of Sohn. Member of the Amsterdam Academy. Gold Medal of Prussia, 1890. Medals at Berlin and Philadelphia. Died, 1886.

No. 37

Winter Sport

13 x 11

KARL HILGERS,   Düsseldorf

Born in Düsseldorf in 1818. Pupil of Düsseldorf Academy; spent some time in Berlin and studied the Dutch and French masters.

No. 38

Holland Interior

23 x 18. Dated 1866

J. A. F. HEYLIGERS,   Antwerp

No. 39

Dutch Market

16 x 13. Dated 1846

BARON HENDRIK LEYS, . Antwerp

Born in Antwerp February 18, 1815, died August 25, 1869. Pupil of
his brother-in-law, F. de Braekeleer, and of Antwerp Academy
under Wappers. Great Gold Medal, Brussels, 1835 ; Paris, 1855
and 1867. Member of the Order of Leopold, 1840; officer of the
same, 1856; commander, 1867; Legion of Honor, 1862; made
Baron in 1862; member of the Brussels Academy, 1845.

No. 40

Far from Home

28 x 21. Dated 1867

ERNST BOSCH, .   Düsseldorf

Born at Crefeld, Germany, in 1834. Pupil in Wesel, of Sehes, Sohn,
Hildebrandt, and Schadow.

No. 22   Girl and Butterfly.
G. Bromley.

No. 5.   The Grandfather's Birthday.
J. P. Hasenclever.

No. 66.   Winter Scene in Holland.
A. Schelfhout.

No. 49.   Forest at Fontainebleau.
Théodore Rousseau.

No. 39. A Dutch Market.
Baron H. Leys.

No. 83. Fruit and Flowers.
Van Haanen.

No. 100. Napoleon. The Return from the Elba.
J. L. H. Bellangé.

No. 41

Bull and Dog

21 x 17. Dated 1838

JACQUES R. BRASCASSAT, Paris

Born at Bordeaux, August 30, 1805, died in Paris, February 27, 1867.
Pupil of Richard and of Hersent. Won the second grand prize for
historic landscape in 1825. Medals, Paris, 1827, 1831, and 1837.
Legion of Honor, 1837. Member of the Institute of France, 1846.

No. 42

The Torturers of Cupid

44 x 36

C. ÉDOUARD DE BEAUMONT, Paris

Born at Lannion, France, in 1821. Pupil of Boisselier. Medals, 1870
and 1873. Member of the Legion of Honor, 1877.

No. 43

The Golden Wedding

44 x 35. Dated 1854

F. DE BRAEKELEER, Antwerp

Born in Antwerp, February 19, 1792. Pupil of Antwerp Academy and
of M. I. Van Brée. Obtained the great prize in 1819, and studied
three years in Rome. Member of the Order of Leopold, and director
of Antwerp Museum. Died, 1883.

No. 44

Autumn's Golden Crown

32 x 20.   Dated 1857

VICAT COLE, R.A.,   .   .   .   *London*

*Born at Portsmouth, England, 1833. Son and pupil of George Cole.
Elected Associate of the Royal Academy, 1870, and Royal Academician in 1880.*

No. 45

Day Dreams

36 x 46.   Dated 1859

THOMAS COUTURE,   .   .   *Paris*

*Born at Senlis (Oise), December 21, 1815, died in Villiers le Bel (Seine-
et-Oise), March 31, 1879. Pupil of Gros and Paul Delaroche.
Won second grand prix de Rome, 1837; medals, 1844, 1847, and
1855. Legion of Honor, 1848.*

No. 46

Russian Landscape, Horses and Figures

60 x 36.   Dated 1867

ADOLPHE SCHREYER, .   .   .   *Paris*

*Born at Frankfort-on-the Main, 1828. Belonging to a distinguished
family, this artist enjoyed every advantage of travel and instruction. In 1855 he followed the regiment commanded by Prince Taxis
to the Crimea, making many spirited studies. Medals, Paris, 1864,
1865, 1867 (Exposition Universelle) ; Brussels Exposition, 1863, and
Vienna Exposition, 1873. Cross of the Order of Leopold, 1864. In
1862 he was made Painter to the Court of the Grand Duke of Meck-
lenburg-Schwerin. Member of the Academies of Antwerp and Rotterdam, and Honorary Member of the Deutsches Nochstift.*

No. 54. Naples (en route à Pompeii).
Oswald Achenbach.

No. 84. Spanish Peasants.
F. M. Eder.

No. 61. A Young Family.
Gustave Sus.

No. 47

The Toast

32 x 24.   Dated 1855

H. D'UNKER, .   . Düsseldorf

Born at Stockholm, May 5, 1829, died at Düsseldorf, March 24, 1866.

No. 48

Landscape, with Horses and Figures

30 x 20

W. VERSCHUUR,   Amsterdam

Born at Amsterdam in 1812, died at Rotterdam in 1874. Pupil of Van Os and C. Steffelaer. Gold medal of the order " Felix Meritis" in 1831; silver medal of the same order in 1822.

No. 49

Forest at Fontainebleau

31 x 21.   Dated 1863

THÉODORE ROUSSEAU, .   . Paris

Born at Paris, 1812. Pupil of Guillon-Lethiere. First exhibited Salon, 1834. Medals, 1834, 1849, 1855. Legion of Honor, 1852. Grand Medal of Honor (Exposition Universelle), Paris, 1867. Died, 1867. Diploma to the Memory of Deceased Artists, 1868.

No. 50

The New Robe

12 x 15.   Dated 1866

ALFRED STEVENS, .   . Paris

Born at Brussels, 1828.   Pupil of Navez in Belgium, and Roqueplan at
Paris.   Medals, Paris, 1853, and at Expositions Universelles of 1855,
1867, and 1878.   Legion of Honor, 1863; officer of same, 1867;
commander, 1878.   Officer of the Order of Leopold; Commander of
the Order of St. Michael of Bavaria; Commander of the Order of
Ferdinand of Austria.

No. 51

Dolce far Niente

18 x 25

HENRI CAMPOTOSTO,   Brussels

No. 52

Vision of Hubertus

32 x 42

THEODORE BUDDE,

No. 6a. Scene in Algiers.
Eugène Fromentin.

No. 34. The Card House.
A. Toulmouche.

No. 73. The Forge in the Tyrol.
F. Zimmermann.

No. 53

The Women and the Secret

(La Fontaine's Fables)

40 x 56.   Dated 1867

HUGUES MERLE,   Paris

Born at Saint Marcellin, France, March 1, 1823. Pupil of Léon Cogniet. Medals, 1861, 1863. Legion of Honor, 1866. Died in Paris, March 26, 1881.

No. 54

Naples (en route à Pompeii)

58 x 40

OSWALD ACHENBACH, . Düsseldorf

Born at Düsseldorf, February 2, 1827. Brother and pupil of Andreas Achenbach. Medals, Paris, 1859, 1861, 1863. Legion of Honor, 1863.

No. 55

Muleteers and Water Carriers of the Alhambra

39 x 60.   Dated 1866

RICHARD ANSDELL, R.A., . London

Born in Liverpool in 1815, died in April, 1885. Self-taught; elected Associate of the Royal Academy, 1861; Royal Academician, 1870. Medal, Paris, 1855.

No. 56

The Christmas Tree

21 x 18. Dated 1864

EDUARD GESELSCHAP, · Düsseldorf

Born in Amsterdam, March 22, 1814, died in Düsseldorf, January 5,
1878. Pupil of Welch and Düsseldorf Academy. Member of Amsterdam Academy.

No. 57

The Zealand Farmer

10 x 13

ADOLF DILLENS,   Ghent

Born at Ghent, January 2, 1821, died there in 1877. Brother and
pupil of Hendrik Dillens. Medals, Brussels, 1848, 1850, 1854;
Paris, 1855. Member of the Order of Leopold, 1862; member of
Amsterdam Academy, 1866.

No. 58

Flowers

18 x 11

GEORGE HARRISON,

No. 38. Holland Interior (Fragment).
J. A. F. Heyligers.

No. 42. The Torturers of Cupid (Fragment).
C. Edouard De Beaumont.

No. 59

Charles IX., Eve of St. Bartholomew

(Painting on porcelain after Baron Wappers)

15 x 19

HOHLE,

No. 60

Landscape

(Pen Drawing)

25 x 18. Dated 1867

JOHANN SCHISCHKIN, St. Petersburg

Born, January 13, 1827, at Jelabuga (Government of Wjatka), Russia. Studied at the Art School in Moscow and at the Academy in St. Petersburg, where he took the great prize in 1863. He is a professor in St. Petersburg, a member of the Academy, and Knight of the Order of Stanislaus.

No. 61

A Young Family

10 x 7

GUSTAVE SUS, Düsseldorf

Born in 1823 at Rumbeck by Rinteln-on-the-Weser. In 1850-51 he was a student at the Academy in Düsseldorf, where later he set up his own studio.

No. 62

Scene in Algiers

18 x 27.   Dated 1857

EUGÈNE FROMENTIN,   Paris

*Born at La Rochelle (Charente-Inférieure), October 24, 1820, died at St.
Maurice, near La Rochelle, August 27, 1876.   Pupil of Rémond and
Cabat.   Visited Algiers in 1846-48 and in 1852-53, and brought
home many sketches, from which he painted his characteristic pictures of Oriental life.   He was the author of a successful romance,
"Dominique" (1863), and admirable works on art.   Medals, 1849,
1857, 1859.   Legion of Honor, 1859; officer of the same, 1869.*

Extracts from Notes Sur les Cent Chefs-d'Œuvres, by M. Albert Wolff.

*In France art lived for a long time on an Orient of imagination, where
violent colors shocked each other in the sunshine and spluttered with
a thousand disorderly fires.   The actual Orient is something quite
different.   The transparence of the atmosphere stretches something
like a tint of silver gray, of exquisite delicacy, over the landscape;
it is soft and harmonious, not violent and showy.   The first time I
watched Stamboul from the bridge of the Bosphorus, at the setting
of the sun, I was surprised at the difference between the Orient
conventional and the Orient of reality.   The first is an agglomera-
tion of violent tints where objects and people are arranged in sil-
houettes on a flame-colored sky; the last is a gentle, penetrating
harmony.   No artist has better rendered the true Orient in its distinction of color than EUGÈNE FROMENTIN.   He was not satisfied
with studying Africa in the products of his predecessors.   He had
seen it with eyes of his own, and estimated it with his personal
thoughts, as a poet with melting heart, an observer with delicate
fidelity.   In this delightful artist the painter's talent was enhanced
by very decided literary aptitude, and thus in his works he not only
paints Africa, he narrates it.*

*The first time I saw a picture by FROMENTIN, at the Salon of 1863, I
think, I was immediately struck by the revelation of the veritable
Orient which the painter had brought for us.   It was the famous*

No. 76. Landscape. Entering the Woods.
B. C. Koek Koek

.

No. 5. The Convalescent.
A. H. Bakker-korff.

No. 78. Winter Landscape—Castle and Figures.
Carl Hilvers.

Arab Falconer, *which the artist exhibited at that period. The horseman was galloping through a wide landscape, carrying a falcon which seemed about to fly. Into that simple scene* FROMENTIN *had contrived to put all the grandeur and all the poetry of African desert scenery and the Arab. The man who could express so many sensations in such a subject was evidently a poet himself, that is to say, a nature sensitive and open to all the seductions of the animated creation. Criticism has often reproached* FROMENTIN *for making too many sacrifices to the literary side of his subjects, that is to say, for having dwelt too much on the anecdote expressed in his pictures. But it is not forbidden in art, that I know of, to tell the world the peculiarities of a distant civilization and put before the public eye its veritable character with a wealth of minute details and with a grand descriptive power. The utmost that can be said of* FROMENTIN *is, that he has spread, here and there, over his own particular Orient, something like a varnish of Parisian elegance; this proceeded rather from the naturally perfect distinction of the man, who conferred on his Arabs the grace of his own individuality. In this delicate artist the brain was fundamentally refined, so that whatever the eye regarded assumed in the thoughts of* FROMENTIN *a poetical cast. Every artist of worth finds it impossible to quite separate his work from his personal sensations. It is really by this that the great painter is distinguished from the artist of secondary rank; the latter is oftenest furnished merely with the painting eye without the artist spirit; he renders marvelously what he can see, without adding the thrill of the soul. Any art work which does not let us likewise look into the privacy of its author remains in an inferior rank, whatever may be the skill of the craftsman.* EUGÈNE FROMENTIN *is revealed from head to foot in his pictures. He was a being of rare distinction, one who ennobled, in some aspect, whatever passed through his mind. He has regarded and painted the Orient like a poet. In his Arab hordes camping in their bivouacs or crossing the desert, he has not chosen to see the reality of things or the details of their degradation; as the hand of the craftsman played over the canvas, the spirit of the artist was careering with a poet's flight through space. When he paints the Arab at rest with his horses browsing untethered beside the tent, he is awed by the mysterious grandeur of such a scene, in the desert silence, under the limpid sky where the stars are shining. When he paints him in action, he perceives him as a manifestation of the tameless restlessness of a wandering historical tribe, a being*

who has never learned to measure and restrain his movements.
He always and everywhere confers upon the creature of the Orient
the real grace, the distinction of the whole race. And the thoughts
of the artist are so overflowing with this subject that frequently he
finds the art of painting inefficient before the burden of all he has to
express. Then he lays down the palette and seats himself at the
table before his inkstand; he writes charming works about the
Orient, where at every line the painter reveals himself through the
man of letters, even as his pictures reveal to us without difficulty
the literary man in the painter.

Those who estimate the value of a work of art from the scale of the
figures used often to blame FROMENTIN for always restricting his
works to small proportions; just as if such and such a tale of
MERIMÉE'S, for instance, was not worth a novel of several volumes
by some one else. But even if we admit that FROMENTIN himself
condemned as inferior his figures of grand dimensions, is it not a
proof of the fine sense of an artist when he recognizes and judges
his own faculty and conforms himself to it? Nor is what is called
grand art always large art. It was not the comprehension of vast
dimensions which this choice spirit lacked. FROMENTIN wrote
about the Masters of Yore, a volume of studies which shows how
thoroughly his mind was open to the grand works of past centuries.
He was content to admire them, without attempting to imitate
them.

No. 63

Landscape and Cattle

32 x 20

JULES DUPRÉ, .   Paris

Born in Nantes, 1812. As a boy he studied design in the porcelain
manufactory of his father, but soon turned his attention to landscape painting, and made his début in the Salon of 1831. Medal,
Paris, 1833. Legion of Honor, 1849. Medal (Exposition Universelle), 1867. Officer of the Legion of Honor, 1870.

No. 80. Corinna Delivering the Martyrs.
F. V. Eugène Delacroix.

No. 90. Skating Scene in Holland.
A. Schelfhout.

No. 71. Easter Morning.

No. 64

Forest at Fontainebleau

16 x 21

N. V. DIAZ DE LA PEÑA, . Paris

Born at Bordeaux, August 21, 1808. His parents were banished from Spain on account of political troubles, and at ten years of age Diaz was left an orphan in a strange country. At fifteen years of age he was apprenticed to a maker of porcelain, where his talent first displayed itself. He quarreled with and left his master, and subsequently spent several years in most bitter poverty. After his ability as a most wonderful colorist was recognized, Diaz painted and sold many pictures, working even too constantly, as if endeavoring by the accumulation of a vast fortune to avenge the poverty of his youth. Medals, 1844, 1846, 1848. Legion of Honor, 1851. Died, from the bite of a viper, November 18, 1876. Diploma to the Memory of Deceased Artists (Exposition Universelle), 1878.

Extracts from Notes Sur les Cent Chefs-d'Œuvres, by M. Albert Wolff.

In the group of painters beyond the average, DIAZ DE LA PEÑA is the great artist of the fantastical. Anything serves him as a pretext for bringing to light his marvelous aptitude as a colorist. He has not the science of ROUSSEAU nor the poesy of COROT, still less the severe grandeur of DUPRÉ. He renders the enchantments of the landscape flooded with sunshine or the forest plunged in luminous twilight, with beams filtering through the thick leafage; he dazzles the eye with all the seductions of a grand colorist; by these obvious qualities, which affect even the uninitiated spectator, he gets closer to the latter than other landscapists of the time. He is the grand virtuoso of the palette, making sport of difficulties. With him everything is of the first impulse; his work is thrown off with brio; the enchantment of the color carries it along. We can imagine him in the solitudes of the forest of Fontainebleau, making the wooden leg resound on the earth and singing with all his lungs to let off his exuberant nature. The countrymen whom MILLET stopped to regard with compassionate thoughts did not attract him. He dots the pond-side, where the sun gleams, with peasant girls, mere little red touches. In his sun-gilt landscapes DIAZ puts such figures as offered, by their costumes, a pretext for the wealth of his palette. The Descent of the Bohemians is the fullest expression of this style; here all is life and air; the band is coming down a steep path; through the foliage the sun rains down its beams and floods the whole picture with a transparent and luminous half-light; it is a perfect dazzle to the eye, like all the works of this great colorist. From the Orient, as he passes through it, he only collects the remembrances of silky stuffs and golden embroideries, spreading forth their pride in the sun; from Italy he only preserves the method of the colorist VERONESE, whom he often equals in the attractiveness, if not in the conception, of his work. As for mythology, it is merely his excuse for modeling in full impasto and in open daylight the nymphs and the Dianas.

DIAZ was above all an improvisator and a creator of fantasies. He himself acknowledged what was lacking in his pictures to place them quite in the first rank. He found himself overflowed with those powers of color which constitute his glory, but to which he sacrificed the rest. Yet we hardly detect the occasional want of completeness in the forms of his figures, so entirely are we under the charm of the color.

The coming on of winter was always dangerous to him. In 1876, DIAZ felt himself attacked by an affection of the chest which rendered all work impossible. He went to Mentone, where for an instant he seemed to revive with a new existence. It was there that he executed his last pictures. Death took him by surprise, still at his work. It was impossible to overcome this character, still full of energy, during the final sickness, unless by taking the brush from his hands and shattering it. Broken at once in frame and in spirit, DIAZ did not resist longer. Without his work, life offered no attraction. From his death-bed, through the open window, he beheld the landscape bathed with sunshine, and the great enchanter died while looking his last on the day-star which inspired all his work.

No. 81. The Syrian Shepherd.
Jean Léon Gérôme.

No. 55. Muleteers and Water Carriers of the Alhambra.
R. Ansdell, R.A.

No. 51. Dolce far Niente.
H. Campotosto.

No. 56. Effect of Autumn.
Théodore Rousseau.

No. 65

Our Little Family

9 x 11. Dated 1867

F. EDUARD MEYERHEIM, . Berlin

Born in Berlin, October 10, 1838, died at Marburg, April 5, 1880. Genre painter, son of Friedrich Eduard Meyerheim. Pupil of Berlin Academy.

No. 66

Winter in Holland

18 x 12. Dated 1858

ANDRÉ SCHELFHOUT, The Hague

Born at The Hague, 1787, died, 1870. Member of all the academies in Holland. Medals in Antwerp, Brussels, Ghent, and The Hague.

No. 67

Landscape

(Pen Drawing)

21 x 14

JOHANN SCHISCHKIN, . St. Petersburg

Born January 13, 1827, at Jelabuga (Government of Wjatka), Russia. Studied at the Art School in Moscow and at the Academy in St. Petersburg, where he took the great prize in 1863. He is a professor in St. Petersburg, a member of the Academy, and Knight of the Order of Stanislaus.

No. 68

Vanity and Modesty

31 x 27

LEONARDO DA VINCI (ATTRIBUTED TO)

No. 69

Les Arabes en Égypt

30 x 18.   Dated 1867

ADOLPHE SCHREYER,   Paris

Born at Frankfort-on-the-Main, 1828. Belonging to a distinguished
family, this artist enjoyed every advantage of travel and instruction. In 1855 he followed the regiment commanded by Prince Taxis
to the Crimea, making many spirited studies. Medals, Paris, 1864,
1865, 1867 (Exposition Universelle); Brussels Exposition, 1863, and
Vienna Exposition, 1873. Cross of the Order of Leopold, 1864. In
1862 he was made Painter to the Court of the Grand Duke of Meck-
lenburg-Schwerin. Member of the Academies of Antwerp and Rotterdam, and Honorary Member of the Deutsches Nochstift.

No. 70

Titian's Daughter

(After Titian)

28 x 35

No. 33.   The Women and the Secret.
Hucues Merle.

No. 71

The Disputed Bonnet

22 x 17. Dated 1866

CHARLES VERLAT, *Antwerp*

Born at Antwerp, 1824. Professor of the Antwerp Academy. Pupil of Nicaise de Keyser. Chevalier of the Legion of Honor.

No. 72

Interior with Figures

16 x 20

VICTOR VAN HOVE, *Paris*

FLORENT WILLEMS, . . *Paris*

Victor Van Hove was born at Renaix, 1825. Member of the Order of Leopold. Medals, in Paris, 1863, and in Vienna, 1873.
Florent Willems was born at Lüttich, January 8, 1823. Medals, at Paris, 1844, 1846, 1855, at Brussels, 1843. Chevalier and officer of the Order of Leopold and Legion of Honor. Medal (Exposition Universelle), 1867; first-class medal (Exposition Universelle), 1878.

No. 73

The Forge in the Tyrol, Winter

40 x 34

RICHARD ZIMMERMAN, *Munich*

No. 74

Easter Morning

46 x 35.   Dated 1868

THEODORE C. SCHUTZ,   Düsseldorf

Born March 26, 1830, at Thumlenjen, by Freudenstadt in Würtemberg. Began with the study of law in the office of a notary, but in 1849-54 studied in the Academy at Stuttgart under Rustige, Neher, and Steinkopf, and painted there the picture which first gave him rep-utation, Confirmation Morning. *In 1854-57 he worked in Munich by himself; but in 1857-63 he entered the Academy and studied under Piloty. After traveling in Italy and Germany, he finally established himself in Düsseldorf.*

No. 75

Cupid's Messages to the Graces

36 x 50.   Dated 1853

L. G. E. ISABEY,   Paris

Born in Paris, July 22, 1804, died in Paris, April 26, 1886. Son and pupil of Jean Baptiste Isabey. In 1830 he accompanied the Expe-dition to Algiers as Royal Marine Painter. Medals, Paris, 1824, 1827, 1855. Member of the Legion of Honor, 1832; officer of the same, 1852.

No. 87. Bohemians.

N. V. Diaz.

No. 47. The Toast.
C. H. D'Unker.

No. 91. Newsians of the Family of Count Egmont, presents to the Execution by the
Duke of Alva.
Baron Égile C. G. Woppers.

No. 76

Landscape, Entering the Woods

50 x 40

B. C. KOEK-KOEK, *Amsterdam*

Born at Middleburg, Zealand, October 11, 1803, died at Cleves, April 5, 1862. Son and pupil of Johannes Hermann Koek-Koek and a student of Amsterdam Academy under Schelfhout and Van Os. Founder of the Academy of Design at Cleves, member of Rotterdam and St. Petersburg Academies, member of the Orders of the Lion and of Leopold; Legion of Honor, 1840. Gold medal at Amsterdam, 1840, Paris, 1840 and 1843.

No. 77

Francis I. at Fontainebleau

60 x 38. Dated 1869

NICAISE DE KEYSER, *Antwerp*

Born at Sandvliet, near Antwerp, August 26, 1813. History and genre painter, pupil of Joseph Jacops and of Antwerp Academy under Van Brée. Great gold medal at Brussels, 1836, Paris, 1840, and medals at almost all exhibitions in Belgium and Holland. Member of the Order of Leopold, 1839; officer of the same, 1855; Bavarian Order of St. Michael, 1851; Order of the Lion, 1844; Commander of the Order of the Oaken Crown, 1857; Swedish Order of the Polar Star; Wörtemberg Crown Order; Legion of Honor, 1862; director of the Antwerp Academy, 1855.

No. 78

Winter Landscape, Castle and Figures

51 x 34

KARL HILGERS, ... *Düsseldorf*

Born in Düsseldorf, 1818. Pupil of Düsseldorf Academy. Spent some time in Berlin and studied the Dutch and French masters.

No. 79

Florentine Flower Girl

38 x 50.   Dated 1867

From a fine specimen of Florentine carving

MICHELE GORDIGIANI,   *Florence*

No. 80

Clorinda Delivering the Martyrs

(From second canto Tasso's "Jerusalem Delivered")

32 x 40

F. V. EUGÈNE DELACROIX, . *Paris*

Born at Charenton St. Maurice, near Paris, April 26, 1799, died in Paris, August 13, 1863. Pupil of Guérin. Exhibited in 1822 his Dante and Virgil, which won him great reputation. Member of the Legion of Honor, 1831; officer of the same, 1846; commander, 1855. Member of the Institute of France, 1857.

Extracts from Notes Sur les Cent Chefs-d'Œuvres, by M. Albert Wolff.

The controlling note in EUGÈNE DELACROIX's painting is the dramatic note. We might say of him that he is the SHAKESPEARE of art; he

No. 8. Stag and Hounds.
J. Melin.

No. 70 "A". The New Shawl.
Unknown.

*has the great author's majesty of conception, his art of painting a
character in a few strokes, and his power of color. That which
interests him is the drama of all epochs, of every literature, and of
every place.* The Bark of Dante *is only the first step, to which suc-
ceed those memorable masterpieces,* The Scio Massacres, Tasso
among the Madmen, The Assassination of the Bishop of Liège, The
Amende Honorable, Jacob Wrestling with the Angel, The Bark of
Christ, Hamlet and the Gravedigger, The Morocco Coast, The Bar-
ricade, The Death of Sardanapalus — *little imports the subject.
Whether he dip in profane or sacred history, in historical anecdote
or in the life of the wild beast, it is the drama and always the
drama which thrills in his magnificent canvases, which inspires
and overcomes us in the contemplation of his works; the drama
which shakes the soul because we feel that the soul of the great
painter is in it; he overthrows us by the sublimity of the present-
ment, the energy of the execution, the magic of his color. In* EU-
GÈNE DELACROIX *genius did not wait for years; it burst forth at
the first stroke, powerful, and, so to speak, in its highest expression.
Here the effort of the start is no mere indication by which to fix a
point of departure. It is the representation of the whole career;
it is as the manifesto, as the programme never departed from, of
a long, glorious artistic reign. In truth, whatever the works to
come shall be like, the first canvas shows their intellectual germ;
what* DELACROIX *occupies himself about, what moves him, is the
drama. The subject is no great thing for this grand artist; it is
naught but a pretext; the dramatic impression proceeding from it
is everything.*

EUGÈNE DELACROIX *had taken from the chilled hands of* GÉRICAULT
*the banner of that revolt which this great genius had raised
against the correct and frigid art born of science, without one throb
of the soul; he carried it proudly and aloft across a hundred battles, to the very end, for the glory of French painting in our century.
He became the chief of the new school, called romantic, of which*
VICTOR HUGO *was the apostle in literature. Like the grand poet,
the illustrious painter was vilified, attacked, and hissed. His art
triumphed, even like* HUGO'S, *over all its opposers. It forced itself
slowly on the public, through innumerable battles. Now it is the
pride of our painting school, as the works of* HUGO *are the radiant
glory of our French nineteenth century literature.*

*His unappreciated masterpieces accumulated in his plain, simple studio,
and the great artist felt no discontent.* DELACROIX *was one of*

those tempered souls who rely for their satisfactions on the secrets
of their work, with an impartial contempt for adulation or for in-
sult. He had arranged his life in his own fashion, and above all,
in such sort that nothing was to disturb him from his art. Ex-
cept a few sparse familiars, to whom were later added the princes
of Orléans, no one could penetrate his existence; even woman's
influence, if it ever colored his life, left no trace there. No one
might boast of having diverted the great artist from his art; no
one ever had empire over him. The flatteries of men and the al-
lurements of women remained equally ineffectual for that iron will,
which would not let itself be indented. It is thus that DELACROIX
was able to leave such voluminous productions. We should be
much deceived if we conjectured that these masterpieces, apparently
executed so freely, had come without effort; they are, on the con-
trary, the result of painful toil and incessant hesitations. If the
artist's pains do not appear in them, they were none the less formi-
dable and often agonizing. Before these admirable productions
hostile routine was obliged to lay down its arms at length. The
renown of DELACROIX ceased not to grow in the midst of the tumult
provoked by his style. The Institute, which had reviled him, com-
prehended that it must needs make a compromise with the master
who contemned it. And now this mutineer, this insurgent, this
revolutionary, is about to enter the Academy. What protests and
what alarms! Annibal ad portas! DELACROIX undertook the siege
of the Academy, and went to seat himself, with a smile on his lips,
among his worst enemies.

The death scene of DELACROIX is of itself an imposing drama. He had
lived alone, and he wished to die in peace. When he felt the su-
preme solution approaching, he directed his faithful housekeeper to
receive no one whatever, sent for a lawyer, and dictated to him his
final will with remarkable calmness and with that lucidity of mind
which only left him with his last sigh. Then he firmly awaited
death, without a shudder, without a complaint, without a regret.
He died self-concentrated, as he had lived, without bravado as
without weakness; neither complaint nor challenge, in the face of
this death which steadily advanced. He passed away in a last
smile, as a man who had well employed his life, and who was sure
that his name would be a possession of posterity.

No. 15. Alpine Landscape.
H. Bürkel.

No. 68. Vanity and Modesty.
Attributed to Leonardo Da Vinci.

No. 81

Syrian Shepherd

33 x 18. Dated 1867

JÉAN LÉON GERÔME, Paris

Born at Vesoul, France, 1824. Went to Paris in 1841, and entered the studio of Paul Delaroche, at the same time following the course of l'École des Beaux Arts. In 1844 he accompanied Delaroche to Italy. He made his debut at the Salon of 1847. In 1853 and 1856 he traveled in Egypt and Turkey, studying closely the history and customs of those countries. Medals, Paris, 1847, 1848, 1855 (Exposition Universelle); Medal of the Institute, 1865; Medal of Honor (Exposition Universelle), 1867; Medals of Honor, 1874; Medal for Sculpture and one of the eight Grand Medals of Honor (Exposition Universelle), 1878. Legion of Honor, 1855; officer of the same, 1867; commander, 1878; chevalier of the Ordre de l'Aigle Rouge, and member of the Institute of France, 1878. Professor in l'École des Beaux Arts.

No. 82

Avenue of Beeches, Winter

48 x 28. Dated 1865

DE MEYER, The Hague

No. 83

Fruit and Flowers

32 x 40. Dated 1861

R. A. VON HAANEN, Vienna

No. 84

Religious Instruction in an Israelitish Household

52 x 38. Dated 1868

KARL HERBSTHOFFER,   .   *Paris*

Born at Presburg, Hungary, April 17, 1821, died in Paris in 1876. Pupil of Vienna Academy under Amerling; went afterward to Paris, where he became naturalized and adopted Isabey's style.

No. 85

Spanish Peasants

64 x 42. Dated 1867

F. M. EDER,   *Seville*

No. 86

Autumn Landscape

22 x 26

THÉODORE ROUSSEAU,   *Paris*

Born in Paris, 1812. Pupil of Guillon-Lethiere. First exhibited, Salon, 1834. Medals, 1834, 1840, 1855. Legion of Honor, 1852. One of the eight Grand Medals of Honor (Exposition Universelle), Paris, 1867. Died, 1867. Diploma to the Memory of Deceased Artists,

No. 75. Cupid's Messages to the Graces.
L. G. E. Isabey.

No. 45. Day Dreams.
Thomas Couture.

No. 31. A Scrapyard.
A. A. E. Hébert.

No. 87

Bohemians

12 x 19

N. V. DIAZ DE LA PEÑA,

Born in Bordeaux, 1808. His parents were banished from Spain on account of political troubles, and at ten years of age Diaz was left an orphan in a strange country. At fifteen years of age he was apprenticed to a maker of porcelain, where his talent first displayed itself. He quarreled with and left his master, and subsequently spent several years in most bitter poverty. After his ability as a most wonderful colorist was recognized, Diaz painted and sold many pictures, working even too constantly, as if endeavoring by the accumulation of a vast fortune to avenge the poverty of his youth. Medals, 1844, 1846, 1848. Legion of Honor, 1851. Died, from the bite of a viper, 1876. Diploma to the Memory of Deceased Artists (Exposition Universelle), 1878.

No. 88

Swiss Peasants, Shrine and Storm

44 x 29. Dated 1867

WILHELM J. REIFSTAHL,   *Berlin*

Born at Neu-Strelitz, 1827. Director of the Art School at Carlsruhe, member of Berlin Academy. Medals at Berlin. In 1848 he made the designs for illustrating "Kugler's History of Art." He traveled much in mountainous countries, and was passionately fond of their scenery.

No. 89

Stag and Hounds

56 x 34.   Dated 1865

JOSEPH MÉLIN,   Paris

*Born in Paris, February 14, 1814. History and animal painter. Pupil
of Paul Delaroche and David d'Angers. Medals, 1843, 1845, 1855,
1858. Died, 1886.*

No. 90

Skating Scene in Holland

47 x 35.   Dated 1849

ANDRÉ SCHELFHOUT,   The Hague

*Born at The Hague, 1787, died 1870. Member of all the academies in
Holland. Medals in Antwerp, Brussels, Ghent, and The Hague.*

No. 91

Neuvaines of the Family of Count Egmont, previous to his Execution by the Duke of Alva

60 x 36.   Dated 1866

BARON É. C. G. WAPPERS,   Antwerp

*Born at Antwerp, 1803, died, 1875. Painter to Leopold I. Pupil of
the Academy of Antwerp and of Herreyns and Van Bree. Officer
of the Legion of Honor. From 1846 to 1853 was director of the
Academy of Antwerp.*

No. 66. "Peasants Bringing Home a Born in the Fields."

No. 6. Norwegian Landscape.
H. F. Gude.

No. 55. Swiss Peasants, Shrine and Storm.
W. Riefstahl.

No. 28. Sunset off the Island Jersey.
Eduard Hildebrandt.

No. 92

Landscape, Cattle and Sheep

53 x 37. Dated 1845

E. J. VERBOECKHOVEN,   *Brussels*

Born at Warneton (West Flanders), July 8, 1799. Medals, at Paris, 1824, 1841, 1855. Legion of Honor, 1845; chevalier of the Orders of Leopold, St. Michael of Bavaria, and Christ of Portugal; decoration of the Iron Cross. Member of the Royal Academies of Belgium, Antwerp, and St. Petersburg. Died, 1881.

No. 93

Elizabeth and Frederic of Bohemia receiving News of the Loss of the Battle of Prague

65 x 42. Dated 1868

CARL VON PILOTY,   *Munich*

Born in Munich, October 1, 1826, died there, July 21, 1886. Son of, and first instructed by, the lithographer, Ferdinand Piloty. Then pupil of Munich Academy under Schnorr, and later under his brother-in-law, Karl Schorn. In 1847 he visited Venice, painted genre pictures and at Leipsic (1840) many portraits, then visited Dresden, where Velasquez became his ideal; went in 1852 to Antwerp and Paris, and thenceforth entered upon the path of Calvinistic realism, to which he owed his great renown. In 1856 became Professor of Munich Academy; from 1874, director of same.

No. 94

"Peasants Bringing Home a Calf born in the Fields"

40 x 32

JÉAN FRANÇOIS MILLET,   Paris

Born at Greville, France, October 14, 1814. Pupil of Mouchel and Langlois, at Cherbourg. His progress there was so remarkable that the Municipality of Cherbourg gave him a small pension that he might go to study in Paris. In 1837 he became a pupil of Paul Delaroche and the friend of Corot, Théodore Rousseau, Dupré, and Diaz. Medals, Paris, 1853, 1864, 1867 (Exposition Universelle). Legion of Honor, 1868. Died, January 20, 1875. Diploma to the Memory of Deceased Artists (Exposition Universelle), *1875. In his whole artistic career Millet only painted about eighty oil paintings, many of which he retained in his studio for a long time, returning to them again and again, in order to satisfy himself.*

Extracts from Notes Sur les Cent Chefs-d'Œuvres, by M. Albert Wolff.

There is no more touching story than that of this great artist, who passed his life in poverty and loneliness. The canvases which now form the glory of French art passed unnoticed at the official Salons, disdained by the juries; the juries exclusively picked out of the Institute, which was omnipotent at that period, and which, though since somewhat transformed, was then in the systematic habit of rejecting the fine and living works which lift so high the art of France. MILLET'S paintings, at first rejected, were afterward admitted at the Salons, but with no success; the artist was reproached for creating ugliness—that is to say, for not painting the conventional peasantry harmoniously shaped and garnished with all the graces. MILLET saw the peasant as a being with round shoulders and hollow chest, from the habit of stooping over the ground; with face and arms baked in the sun and tanned by

No. 69. Les Arabes en Égypte.
Adolphe Schreyer.

No. 91. The Christmas Fair.

the wind. In those deathless masterpieces of his, the peasant appears in the majestic verity of the human creature wrestling with the earth, which he impregnates and makes to live. But there came no awards from the Salon, no pay, no sort of encouragement, with the exception of the bravos of certain youthful artists and the applause of some rare art critics, who gradually rallied to the side of this original genius. Through every kind of neglect MILLET pursued his road, with head high and ironical lip. He had on his side the approbation of those whom he esteemed the most—DELACROIX, ROUSSEAU, DUPRÉ, COROT, DIAZ, and of that other great artist so long overlooked, BARYE. The common struggle had established something like a brotherhood of arms among all these pioneers. The little group marched hand in hand against superior numbers—the whole sleek mediocrity of art—as a handful of heroes marches to fight a numerous army, with the determination to conquer or die. Of all those fine artists MILLET alone was not to know success. His destiny was cruel to the end; he fell mortally wounded in the combat, at the hour of the others' triumph. When, finally, after such tedious struggles and such sickening toil, his art began to be talked of, the painter, struck down by sickness, had lost his strength and energy. We may say of MILLET that he died of his genius, conquered before his time, fallen to earth at the moment when age was only just foreseen, an age that would have been gentle and happy; and that he left to posterity, which restores the balance of all things, the care of keeping his name as that of one of the greatest in French art.

Little by little, from the habit of identifying himself with the men of the fields, MILLET had himself become a peasant. Tall in stature, with powerful shoulders, with a face sun-browned but full of character, dressed in poor clothes and with wooden shoes on his feet, he might have been taken for a plowman. In the peasants of his works we find again the artist himself; he claimed to have got into his painting that which he called the cry of the earth, and the "ugh!" of the digger whose chest was crushed between his strokes. We might say, too, that MILLET got into his painting the cry of art, and the sob of the grand painter condemned to live in privation.

Notwithstanding, before his death MILLET could see advancing toward him the step of justice, the never-dying, the eternal laggard. When for the first time, at the Exposition of 1867, the public saw a number of his works brought together in one spot, they were struck by the variety of that art which till then had been called monotonous.

A first-class medal was designed to be thrown to this grand genius,
who, since the Salon of 1853, had not carried off any prize; there
was even added, to do honor to the order, rather than the recipient,
the ribbon of the Legion of Honor, which, after thirty years of
noblest toil, was to be the consolation of this illustrious man, a
martyr to every kind of affliction. When MILLET died, at sixty
years, in that village of Barbizon where all his humble and re-
signed existence was passed, the Government manifested some
shame at having left the illustrious artist so long in abandonment.
It offered his widow a small pension. It is not seemly to insist too
much on the poor question of money when we count up the labors of
a man who set disdainfully aside the considerations of success to be
able to live only in his art.

One day, while talking with me of the period of poverty which the
artists of his generation had passed through, ROUSSEAU said:

" We were always without a sou, but we never spoke of money, for
money counted for nothing in our ambition."

When we speak of MILLET, it is more seemly, again, to touch lightly on
the question of prices, which prove nothing. The Man Hoeing,
which represents a fortune, is no greater a work to-day than at the
period when the great artist sold it for two thousand francs. The
years of wretchedness which MILLET passed through will be redeemed by the centuries of imperishable glory which await his
name in the future. The humble thatched cottage of Barbizon, where the life of MILLET flowed along, pertains to history
more than the rich mansion of a fortunate man in easy circum-
stances, where the stone stands generally unhallowed and un-
speaking, without a recollection of the being whose life has slipped
through it.

No. 95

Holy Family

62 x 76. Dated 1868

FELICE SCHIAVONI,   Venice

No. 31. Evening Landscape.
Adolphe Weber.

No. 99. Battle of the Fists (Fragment).
Peskoff.

No. 10. The Musical Schoolmaster (Fragment).
F. De Braekeleer.

No. 96

The Colza Gatherers, Effect of Sunset with New Moon

50 x 28. Dated 1868

JULES ADOLPHE BRETON, . Paris

Born at Courrières, France, May 1, 1827. Pupil of Drölling and of Dévigne. Medals, London, Vienna, and Brussels, and at Paris in 1855, 1857, 1859, 1861. Legion of Honor, 1861. Medal of the First Class, and officer of the Legion of Honor (at Exposition Universelle), 1867. Medal of Honor (Salon), 1872. Knight of the Order of Leopold, 1881. Ribbon of St. Stanislaus of Russia. Corresponding Member of the Academies of Vienna, Stockholm, and Madrid.

No. 97

Luther, Wife, Children, and Melancthon

64 x 50. Dated 1867

(Perhaps only example of the artist in this country)

G. A. SPANGENBURG, Berlin

Born at Hamburg, 1828. Royal Professor and member of the Berlin Academy; also member of Vienna and Hanau Academies. Medals at Cologne, Berlin, and Vienna. In 1849 went to Antwerp Academy for a short time; in 1851 went to Paris and remained six years; studied a short time under Couture. At the National Gallery, Berlin, are his Luther Translating the Bible and The Procession of the Dead. His picture of Luther with his Family is at the Museum at Leipsic, and has become well known from the engraving by Louis Schulz.

No. 98

Landscape and Cattle, Approaching Storm

62 x 44. Dated 1859

CONSTANT TROYON,   *Paris*

Born at Sèvres, 1810. His parents wished him to be a painter of porce-
lain, but, after a time spent in the manufactory at Sèvres, he studied
under Riocreux, and became a painter of landscapes and animals.
Medals, Paris, 1838, 1840, 1846, 1848, 1855. Legion of Honor, 1849.
Member of the Amsterdam Academy. Died, 1865. Diploma to the
Memory of Deceased Artists (Exposition Universelle), *1878.*

Extracts from Notes Sur les Cent Chefs-d'Œuvres, *by M. Albert Wolff.*

Counted in this admirable group of painters, which throws such luster
on French art, are men of foremost rank in every style. Historical
painters, character painters, landscape painters, imaginative
painters, men of fantasy and men of mind, technists of the palette
and single-hearted observers of nature—all these men form in their
assemblage a kind of quintessence of the art-spirit of France. In
these rapid sketches the reader has successively seen what kind of
second and third-rate professors have secured in the eye of history
the glory of attending to the early lispings of our heroes. The
latter, without exception, formed themselves by the direct contact
of nature, not till after having shaken off the influences which
weighed upon their unfortunate youth. I have named, one by one,
the subalterns charged with the primary artistic education of
these painters, all destined to show the mark of genius in one kind
or another. The first instructor of TROYON *was named* RIOCREUX,
a feeble light, like all those pretenders who thought they could sub-
due to their own glimmer the great stars which were rising over
French art. Like JULES DUPRÉ, *the grand animal painter* TROYON
passed his first youth in a porcelain factory; like that fine land-
scapist, he played the prelude to his glory with just the kind of

No. 96. " The Gleaners"—Effect of Sunset with New Moon.
Jules Adolphe Breton.

No. 3. The Consultation.
W. Sohn.

No. 1. Confidence.
Florent Willems.

No. 2. The Young Mother,
J. B. J. Trayer.

work which contradicts grand art by its timorous industry. The superb executant of innumerable masterpieces grew pale over his dishes until the day when he divined his real mission and took his flight.

CONSTANT TROYON was not twenty years of age when he bade an eternal farewell to the Sèvres factory. Where should he go? Straight ahead, without any settled course; everywhere that Nature revealed herself to his young intelligence he made halt. When he felt hungry, he offered his services to the first potter whom he encountered on his route, and as soon as he had earned a few weeks' freedom at this humble toil, he grasped again his staff and his color-box and marched farther on. Now workman and now artist, he appealed in this fashion to the modest task-work of the china painter for the means to await the day when he should be a real artist.

Thus we find for all these men the same kind of boyhood, disturbed by the struggle for the daily crust. With the exception of DELACROIX and COROT, they were all forced to conquer from privation the right to shed the loftiest artistic glory over their native land. TROYON, for his part, only caught at a rather late date the perception of his true pathway. There is nothing in his first manner which could make us foresee the rank he was one day to assume; his paintings bore trace for many years of the painful labor of designing on porcelain, as the slave who has fought out his liberty carries the scars of the bamboo which used to plow his flesh. It needed ten years of TROYON'S life to make him forget what had been taught him as a lad; it was only little by little and very slowly that the artist was able to rid himself of the influences of his teaching at Sèvres.

Success came hesitatingly and painfully. Not to speak of his early landscapes, which do not count in his achievement, the most important canvases passed unnoticed. Life was hard for the young landscape painter. COROT, ROUSSEAU, JULES DUPRÉ, DIAZ, and DAUBIGNY marched in the van of the movement. Through the splendors, still disdained, of their painting, MILLET would throw off a landscape, from time to time, in a note of severity and melancholy. TROYON joined in the step, as a conscript takes the road behind a squad of veteran soldiers. The first years of the painter were dogged by poverty, which saturated his spirit with a bitterness from which it never got free. Arrived later, by the evolution of his style, to renown and wealth, TROYON preserved the gloom of

these humble beginnings. In this he was at fault. Did he not
share the public neglect with the first landscape painters of the
age? Had he *suffered more, and more* unjustly, than the chiefs *of*
his company? *And then, if I must express my full opinion, would*
the canvases of *TROYON, as a landscapist, grandly* brushed as
they are, have sufficed to establish *his high renown?* It was
accident and a journey to Holland which *revealed* to TROYON his
true mission, that of an animal painter of the first rank, sup-
ported, this time, by a landscapist of very great talent, but not the
equal of the masters.

With this development of the artist, which promptly gave him his rank,
success came to him rapidly. At a distance of two centuries
TROYON continued the traditions of the celebrated Dutch animal
painters without imitating them. PAUL POTTER was to find a suc-
cessor worthy of him. In his journey into Holland, TROYON had
studied the works of the grand master, and he took his line at once.
Why had he not perceived before that the art of the animal painter
offered inexhaustible resources to his rare endowments as a colorist, while it still allowed him to remain a landscapist of lofty
value?

The great technical skill of *TROYON, his matchless control of* his craft,
allowed him to grapple with *all the effects of nature*. In one of his
subjects, exhibited among *the Hundred Masterpieces he has painted*
a rainbow struck out from clouds charged with electricity, while on
the other side the *torrents of sunshine falls* upon a grand red spotted
heifer enjoying the warm rays. *The* Cow at the Drinking Place,
with The Valley of the Toucques, or The Ferry, are so many masterpieces of the style bespeaking TROYON'S vivid power, his enthrall-
ing charm as a colorist.

This new line, then, began the true career of TROYON, which was to
make him so illustrious. Money commenced to pour in, too, along
with honor, yet without consoling the painter for the poverty and
neglect of the past. Bitterness became one of his habits, and he
made his years of experiment responsible for their gropings and
the difficulty of his quest; his mind always dwelt on his earlier
times, when he used to sit drawing on the side of the road, cursing
the heartless fate which was always calling him off from his art
dream to involve him in the struggle for daily bread. Arrived at
the height of his position, the little china painter of yesterday never
could forgive the troubles of the former years; they were always
coming up in his conversation, with a strongly marked resentment

No. 98. Landscape and Cattle—A Coming Storm.
Constantine Troyon.

No. 78. Interior with Figure.
Victor Van Hove and Florent Willems.

*No. 79. Titian's Daughter, after Titian.

toward his epoch. In this, TROYON, in fact, showed himself
simply what he was, the painter whose qualities were closed up in
his art, and who outside of art had not the balanced character
capable of looking at things from aloft. Personally I had not the
advantage of knowing the famous animal painter, but I learn from
the friends who lived with him that TROYON, beyond his painting,
could bring no philosophy of discernment to his views of life. It
was useless to try to comfort him in praising extravagantly the
splendid position he had attained; he carried the conversation in-
cessantly back to his days of penury, and he frankly advanced the
idea that his contemporaries only redeemed a small part of their
wrongs toward him (TROYON) in overwhelming him now with
gold and honors.

Undoubtedly it would have been more dignified, and even more just, to
refrain from traveling eternally over those years of effort; but so
was TROYON constituted. It was his nature to dwell on a fixed
idea; the recognition coming from all quarters was only his due;
he could not put it to the credit of his contemporaries; he had been
so long in the struggle that he fancied success and prosperity
might again leave him in the lurch. We might even discover, perhaps, at the bottom of this morbid nature an exaggerated attribu-
tion of genius to himself. It was thus that he took measures in his
lifetime for assuring his name an immortality in establishing a
prize, bearing the name of TROYON, and pledging to the successful
competitor among the young animal painters the means of working
in peace for a term of years.

Over the death of TROYON there has been formed a legend pretending
that he was killed by disease resulting from the poverty of his
youth. There is no truth in this. The admirable painter of animals had only to blame his own exacting temperament if death
mowed him down toward his sixtieth year, when all the other grand
artists, whose sufferings had been as sore and even greater than his
own, were forgetting the first troubles with the first success. A
man does not die of poverty after he has finally bidden it farewell
for more than twenty years. TROYON died comparatively young
because his temperament killed him by overreaching itself in everything, good as well as evil. He worked too much and tormented
himself too much; he indulged himself more than was proper with
the joys of life; and that is the reason he died at an age when, with
more self-balance, he might have seen before him long years of pro-
duction and celebrity.

No. 99

Battle of the Fists before Ivan the Terrible

74 x 52. Dated 1863

PESKOFF, .   St. Petersburg

FISTIC COMBAT DURING THE REIGN OF CZAR JOHN THE TERRIBLE

"*These fistic combats were performed under the reign of the Czar John the Terrible, in his presence, to entertain his subjects.*

"*The famous Terebejewitsch, favorite of the Czar, had taken the liberty to offend the wife of Kalaschnikoff, a merchant, when she was going home from church. She rid herself of him, ran home, and informed her husband as to what had happened.*

"*The following day the fistic combat would take place; Kalaschnikoff was resolved to fight with Terebejewitsch. The painting represents the moment where Terebejewitsch has already had a combat, and is expecting a new combatant. Kalaschnikoff steps forward, and, though detained by the entreaties of his wife, is resolved, for the honor of his wife, to fight with Terebejewitsch for death or life. The merchant, Kalaschnikoff, killed Terebejewitsch, but was afterward hanged by the command of the Czar, for having slain his favorite.*

"*On the tribune is the Czar sitting with his attendants. At the right of the picture are the relations of the killed combatant. At the left side the fools of the Czar are sitting one upon another; beside them are the musicians, and between them, standing a little higher, a man holding up a cup, the prize for the victor.*"

No. 100

Napoleon.   The Return from Elba

75 x 60. Dated 1864

J. L. H. BELLANGÉ,   .   .   .   Paris

Born at Paris, February 16, 1800, died there, April 10, 1866. History and genre painter; pupil of Gros and of the École des Beaux Arts.

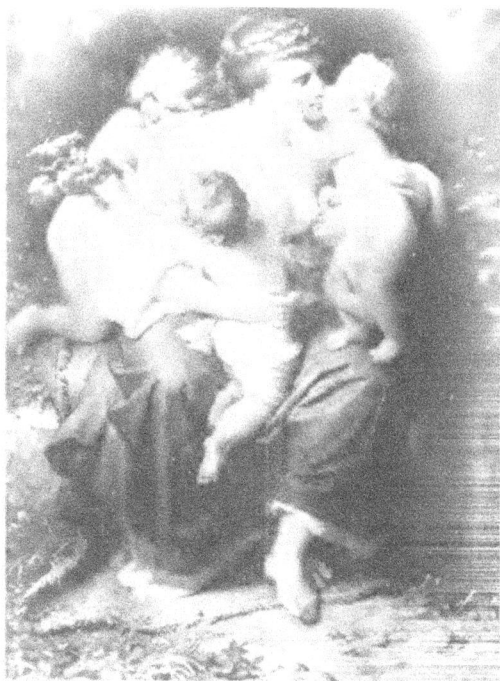

No. 11. Confidence.
C. Pérus.

No. 16. The Happy Mother.
D. Bloch

No. 63 Landscape and Cattle.
Jules Dupré.

Exhibited in nearly every Salon from 1822 to 1866. Medals, 1824.
1855. Member of the Legion of Honor, 1834; officer of the same.
1861. Director of the Rouen Museum, 1837-54.

No. 101

Large Roman Mosaic

58¼ x 31¼

No. 102

Mother Love

52 x 78. Dated 1868

WILHELM VON KAULBACH, Munich

Born at Arolsen, October 15, 1805. Pupil of Düsseldorf and Munich
Academies, under Cornelius. In 1849 appointed director of Munich
Academy. He was an officer of the Legion of Honor; Grand Com-
mander of the Order of St. Michael; Commander of the Order of
Francis Joseph, and Corresponding Member of the Institute of
France and of several academies. Died in Munich, April 7, 1874.

AMERICAN ART ASSOCIATION,
Managers.

THOMAS E. KIRBY, Auctioneer.